dead beats

"Beautiful Mel Torme" was published in *City Lights: An Anthology of Poetry and Art*. "Learning with Whiskey" was published in the *Ibbetson Street Review*. "Dead Respectability" was published in *Citi*.

Edited by Florella Orowan

Photo of Sam Cornish on p. 20 by Jerome Bowman.

All other photographs by Sam Cornish: p. 9, Druid Hill Avenue, Baltimore, 1990s; p. 10, Roxbury (Boston), MA, 1980s; p. 14, Boston night, 1980s; p. 18, downtown Boston, 1980s; p. 24, Orson Welles Cinema, Cambridge, MA, 1970s; p. 30, Dudley Station, Roxbury (Boston), MA, 1970s; p. 35, Boston, 1990s; p. 41, Boston alleyway, 1970s; p. 46, central California, 1990s.

ISBN 978-0-9795313-6-1

Designed by
FLAR Design
Allston, MA 02134

Published and distributed by
Ibbetson Street Press
25 School Street
Somerville, MA 02143
617-628-2313

9 8 7 6 5 4 3 2 1
First Edition

For Bill Corbett, Elmer Bernstein and Dale Patterson

—friends in poetry

Master, we have toiled all night and have taken nothing.

— Luke 5:5 (KJV)

dead beats

Poems by Sam Cornish

Ibbetson Street Press

Contents

MY YOUNG AMERICA

These were the days of my young
America in the pages of City Lights

and the *Evergreen Review*
Allen Ginsberg recalling the days

of his naked youth being policed by *Time*
Magazine the lovers of J Edgar Hoover

America Sacco and Vanzetti
the Scottsboro Boys rotting

in history Ginsberg lost
in his poems

trying to find the country he discovered
in the lies passed on like hand me downs

from one brother to another
by the Founding Fathers   Beat memories

of beautiful boys (Allen and Peter on the cover
of *Evergreen Review*)   there they are

Allen and Peter a letter to the world
in love with each other and the country

that loved them in *Life Magazine* naked underground
poetics   what you saw was what you got

two beautiful boys   America giving
you the finger

THE MODERN AGE

William Carlos Williams sawbones good
Dr. of the English

of uptown   downtown   called
today

the inner city
ghetto by intellectuals

of the fifties (now the 'hood)
in his poems

wrote and read
'bout old colored women Negro

men God he hated
the modern age

like a drink before noon (too early
for me) where is old King Cotton

when you need some bossin'
the sun

that never set
on a Negro in this town

CASSADY

barber's boy
writes

"Uncle Sam's
no relative of mine"

broke in Kansas
hungry in Kansas

horny in Kansas
alone in the West

Buick and Plymouth
my home

hitchhiking
writer & drunk

cowboy
of the Denver

bus stop
and barber

shop
letter writer

of the eternal
sentence

and blank
verse poets

rode

out of flophouses
into America

driving
stolen cars

lookin' for chicks
and Keroauc

BOOGIE

for Cora Cook

cousin Cora
can boogie
down to her knees
rap the floor
shake hips
and mean no harm
cousin Cora
got so much
heart
she don't know
where
to put it

O BURNING ANGEL

for Stanley Kramer

in my veins
in my heart

wild one
of the road

in leather
chewing

gum
Marlon Brando

o burning
angel

of the
highway

eating the dirt
of little towns

like these

MY MAN

the jazz
man beats

his drum
like he whips

his women   his
black face

purple
with rage

my jazz man
with his

nigger
face

wants to
marry

me my horn
player

jazz man
plays   a sunny

day
something bad

blows
his horn

like he
got

his thing
in me

his music
is the

jungle

in the city

bars
stompin'

his blues
into me

HITCHING

Jack
Kerouac's

on a roll

and he's   not
stopping

for commas
semi-colons

and paragraphs

period

LAFAYETTE SQUARE

I used to walk at night
I thought
I was a young Thomas
Wolfe reading every book
in the neighborhood library
the paperback in my dresser
drawer   four-eyed Jack Beans
(that's me)
too cheap to buy a pair of shoes
always a nickel for the paper   used
books today I read Owen Wister
saw the sturdy horses the lean
men cowboys men that ride
instead of walk unless it's down
the middle of the dusty western
street tonight in Harlem square
my hand just above my hip
I owned the night
(and never gave it back)
my writing
done the city gone
to rest I was
the Virginian and Thomas Wolfe   their
prose and poetry written and read
I was lost and by the wind griefed and
my name was Thomas Wolfe

LANGSTON KNOCKING

to Vincent Dorio, with appreciation

poems (one day)
will come
(I promise)
for you
Langston Hughes (head
full of rivers)
sorrow
Georgia
pine
and a little
moon
shine jazz
give the feet (a little
                    jive)
a snap
                    to the fingers
corn rows
                    and red
shoes
with toes
          (better
to keep the
beat)
                    that Bourbon
Street R&B
                    like
today
a poem
will come

and open

a door
say
come in

we have
been waiting
for you   for Langston
a poem will come to you
and you
and you   I promise

NEAL

Cody of the pool hall
and backwoods

like Gene Autry
of the Hollywood

West the sunset
and horse

the gasoline
station

on his tombstone
he wanted to be

an Indian fighter
George Washington

Daniel Boone
in a coonskin cap

and here he is
shouting

"go go go go"
to Negroes

and bop
stolen cars

lookin' for chicks
and Kerouac

THE BIG KILL

for Mickey Spillane and Harold Sock

the real
blonde

is opening
her

white silk
blouse

one button
after another

in front
of a hard

boiled
dick

in a trench
coat

his gun
is pointed

at her
waist

he wants
the truth

it is right
there

in front

of him
he says

my gun
is quick

and I
am the jury

tonight

BALTIMORE IN THE SPRING

sometimes after work strolling
along the white side of town

and listening
to Sinatra

crooning
What is America

to me
but he has the world

on a string
and you almost see him

sway
fingers

snapping   so cool
in his suit   thin

tie   it breaks the heart
the young

children
in the front yards

schools closed
for the day the women

in the windows chatting
on these side streets

where the Polish live
in Baltimore

there are narrow
sidewalks clean-

swept
the women are home

in the afternoon

the old

man at work
a butcher cop working men

breadwinners the flower boxes

lined up
in the window

sills these streets close
to the Negro

streets are almost
friendly

now and then someone
behind a door

hidden by a low
hanging shade or curtain

calls me a coon
so softly

almost whispered I smile
I know

this is Baltimore
and spring

has just begun

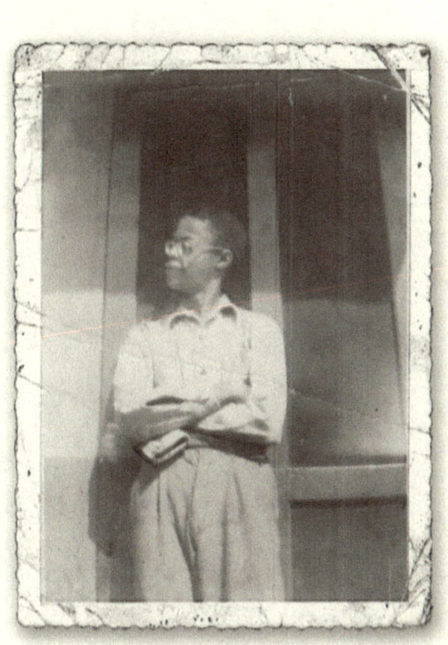

LANGSTON HAS HIS HARLEM

on the typewriter
keys

on Lenox Avenue
and after hours

men
and women   jazz

and the soul
in Louis Armstrong's

horn
Bessie Smith

song   trouble
in Billie's life

a country
of my own

Langston your Harlem
is what you have given

me

THE DEAD LECTURER IS DOWN
Amiri Baraka in the 1960s

for Roger Tazwell, dead poet

LeRoi
        is a
street
        poem
going
        by
a little
        jig in his

        step
his legs

break
        at the
knee
        ready
for a tap

dance
        his jive
is cool

and
        talkin'
baby
        (not
a child
        or woman)
man
        he says
what's
        up
baby
        Roi
is going
        by

KISS ME

for Henry Hathaway and Alfred Newman

Richard Widmark laughed
crazy man

coughed into a handkerchief
sweated

in a heavy overcoat black shirt
white tie a sharp

dresser
like a Nigger pimp

treat (he says)
a broad with a swift belt

across her chops
then slip a sawbuck

into her blouse
pat   her on the buns

man he was
all   dough

from robbin' banks (no liquor
stores or old ladies'

pension checks)
Richard knocked

off banks (took only
rich folks' money)

F.B.I.
bullets ripped

through his overcoat
bit

holes
into his suit

and he bled
all over

his white shirt
and took forever

to die

YOUNG LEROI ON THE NEW AMERICAN POETICS

to Frank Harris

a poem is bull
                              shit
walking
                    talking

writers
                    whose words are
Jim Crow
          laws

                    all Negro faces
are
          either
Toms   or razors
                    from
jive   ass
                              dudes
striding
                              in platform shoes
young LeRoi
                              is a mirror
to the world   in

which white people
looked   young LeRoi is
                              going gone

MILES DAVIS

to his left
a woman

he turns
like a cat

to play
"Bitches'

Brew"
a genius

he is like
a school

boy taking
his marbles

and going
home

BORN TO KILL WITH BEDROOM EYES

Of dark music for the movies

For Bill Corbett, lover of the hard-boiled stuff
and Roy Webb, composer of music for B-films

he is born to kill with bedroom eyes   flesh pots
with harlot's mouths   the puffed up lower lip
the blonde with the scarlet   mouth the blues eyes
looking for trouble   and a little fun
a drink on the house   straight up woman
hash slinger man trap   and streetwalker
gave the nuns a hard time   and now she's givin'
it back to rock jaw   greasy kid stuff
in his hair   second rate Dillinger
Lawrence Tierney in Reno   don't fuck with me
fellow* he will roll   the dice for a smile
slap it off her face   wipe her tears
(much later)
with a handkerchief   from his upper suit pocket
he's a soft touch
for a dame   in his nigger-
shined shoes   stands six foot four
of bartender wrestler   and drunk
knocking over candy stores   hitting the poor
box he   is her kind of man
with the bedroom eyes   women fight for him
in nightmares   and filling stations
and divorce courts   a man who knows
what he wants is you

**Joan Crawford, every day of her life*

WAITING TABLES

for Maritta Wolfe

she's tough and calls
you honey

balancing trays
of steaks

pork chops
ribs

and meat
loaf

fried foods
bad

for you good
to eat wash

down with Coors
and Rolling

Rock   gravy
like grease

in a cold pan
these women

are slamming
and sliding

meat and
count the peas

and broccoli
on tables and you

don't talk
back   twenty

per cent and

thank you
does not

pay the rent

YOU NEVER KNOW ABOUT THE WINTER

for Margo Lockwood

the only poor we know
are beside us

in the long lines waiting
for coffee in the mornings

seven and ten an hour men
and women waiting like I do

for a scratch ticket the numbers
and the late night news

the lottery
school a better life for the children

we did not plan on having
the stork never heard of condoms

and the Holy Mother is busy sometimes
in other neighborhoods our parish

is poor the collection plate
is passed from one good

man to another
and we do the best we can

we are the poor they don't talk
about our streets

for now our wives
are working and the dollar menu

is good and steady
our teachers say the kids are learning

and there are jobs and the poor we know
but you never about know

about the winter
till it comes

but we are the people of the neighborhoods
this what we are and this is what we have

AMERICAN SWEETHEART

for Martin Rodriguez, who loves strong mean bitches

whatever happened to Baby Jane
in her flip flops takin' a drag

on a filter tip Kools
scraping the floor hanging on

to the icebox door with an Oreo
and a bottle of beer   kitchen

in a whirl   feeling so good talking
to light bulbs and cockroaches

child actor
America's sweetheart

has-been   the tap dancing
white kid with the finger curls

bloodshot eyes in a house
dress   three days old smelling

of piss   whatever happened
to you Baby Jane   who used to keep

America warm in those hungry
depression days dancing

up the plantation stairs
my little southern gal   our little

chile you were tomorrow
little sugar girl of

a dustbowl black storm time
singing of hope beyond Kansas

THE BLUES HE GOT

for Blind Lemon

boys
        sing
                the blues

        like a Negro

                if it is
                        just a song

        the
                blues
                        man
                                is
                                        life
                                                guitar

                                                        pickin'
                                words
                                        the blues
        he got
                is his

life
        an ol' nigger thing

GENTLEMAN JUNKY

William Burroughs "fag
from the Big Apple"

dressed like the heat
Dennis O'Keefe in "T-Men"

Mark Stevens in "The Street
With No Name" in your trench coat

sloppy dresser in a film
noir Alan Ladd

with your razor-sharp wit
an FBI Hoover fruit

looking for counterfeiters
a suit hustling slot machines

hookers and a nigger
whore's America and sheriff's badge

William Burroughs   you are not the fuzz

BEAUTIFUL MEL TORME

for Frank Miller, in loving memory

The drummer
                sits above
                the horn
and us
is the Left   Bank
        the music
        jumping
        over heads
and April
        in Paris

is a pretty   Mel Torme

smooth and crooning
                a foggy day
and there is nothing
a tune   from memory
of an old record
                you may talk
                about the blues
                (and this is jazz)

cause hearing it ain't the same
as playing it
                live

says/beats
                the drummer

LEARNING WITH WHISKEY

for Jim and Joanne Randall

drinking with Jim
without getting drunk
holding on to each word
this is a classroom
with beer chasers
open your head
like a book
you have never read
before
listen to him
talk paragraphs
his school is straight up
the drunks
are nodding
in the afternoon
they have
kept the bar stools warm
for us listen
to Doreski
I am here to read Creeley LeRoi
and Tate
what it is
Bowles and Burroughs
to be white
and beat
the importance of a red
wheelbarrow
drinking with Jim
school begins at three
two hours before happy
hour

GETTING A LIFE
Remembering Robert Creeley

for David Franks

at book signings
in his slim

poems
with the words

left
out   the truth

on the floor
like scenes cut

from a movie
you miss them

there is nothing
to hold the

poem together
but his breath

in the mike
before

the audience
holding

on to every
spoken word

and hearing
nothing

THEY USED TO STEAL HIS BOOKS

reading
poetry on a stool

in a coffee house*
between

folk singers Jim
and Jean

is like having
a conversation

with a piece
of paper

you are a fag
they say

whispering
as polite people

do uncool no
Ginsberg a drunk they said

reading
like he was in New York

he's frisky
with his hands above

his nasty head for an audience
for free drinks the hat passed

around his friends fellow
poets not a nickel

bag among them he's gone now
but you can find him

online if you can
afford it

* *The Fog Horn, a coffeehouse in Baltimore in the 1960s*

DEAD RESPECTABILITY

the poet looking for cigarette butts
in the gutters of Common

wealth Avenue is not a bum living alone on Joy
Street   he's John Wieners

his friends in poetry will speak well
of him after he's dead   at MIT the Blacksmith reading

reciting

but see him now and then
out of his fucking mind

he will be okay he's dying his poems are collected
in a signed limited edition

that poets cannot afford
they will thumb

through the paperback
edition at the Grolier Poetry Bookshop

(nothing sells like the classics) and the best books are
the review copies

the books you never pay for   good
hunting Mr. Wieners

the downtown and uptown
gutters are littered with cigarette butts

like the shelves of poetry
collections in Barnes and Noble

waiting for Wieners wanting a true poem
life not literature he wrote letters

in poems   small press editions
read in coffee shops and storefront bookshops

to lovers of poetry
and his work

to cigarette-smoking unwashed
assholes for Negro rights and peace

fags beating bongos the *New American*
Poetry on mimeograph queer

is good John Wieners Frank O'Hara poems are
looking for you (kid) on Forty-Second

Street in the all night movie
bathroom dollar hotel rooms where you

stretch out your arms touch the walls
in a single cot long room

(and wish you stayed in Baltimore
the only Negro poet)

downtown drinking Thunderbird National
Bohemian Beer finger typing   like Roi and Creeley

for love of the people the common language
of the stoops and avenue

the Negro night and jazz
in your fingers to the keys

of the typewriter
fresh out of the pawnshop

next to the bed a plate
of kale last night's cigarettes (like Ray Milland in "The Lost
Weekend")

and all those Totem Corinth poetry
books from the Eighth Street

Bookstore where you saw Ginsberg
so cool like he's here

right now in this room
in New York talking poetry reading poems

and you can't believe that he sounds like
another guy like you reading

his stuff like the words are from somewhere
on Druid Hill Avenue in Baltimore

in a cheap unheated apartment
where the streets are always night

dangerous punks
winos he's trying to save

America with a poem and chanting
and the world

is so small that Kruschev and Nixon
the cops are here in this room

waiting for Wieners and O'Hara to walk in
without knocking

the underfed non-educated Negro generation
the post-slavery depression World War II

Negro in the police station Ginsberg
white jazz post America of a beat America

of *Time Magazine* the Communist intellectual
American life afraid to be men   the

book-loving Negro Huck Finns white four-eyed faggots
in American name only

Eisenhower schoolhouse door free South
separate and even the black

eye popping knee-knocking stolen by
Elvis imprisoned in the living room life

John Wieners there you are a nigger like me
a poet without a butt a smoke

a coffee house bard in Boston who remembers
Lamont Cranston the clouding

of the mind Mae West more man
than Cary Grant (see her upstairs

pretending to be a woman) the tits
are hers the body is Wallace Berry

John Wieners middle age is for
the empty nest wasp you're my St. Peter

on speed   it's "hard work if you can get it"
if you are Jimmy Cliff in Harvard Square

IF OLD COLLECTIBLES COULD TALK

Kerouac beat the bongos
here Ginsberg wandered

those bright young men
of the fifties like me and

the man in the fedora
pulled low the man

in the rain the killer
beside you twenty

five and expenses
chain-smoking with an eye for tall

blondes a shot glass away
with a long old story

and you're not going
anywhere bartender

everything is on me
Philip Marlowe dick

and shamus gumshoe with the bottle
in the lower drawer of his desk

deadbeat bum and drunk
cold long legged blond

when the rent is due ducking
the landlord and landlady

it's a paperback original's dream
the jokes are not funny   Marlowe cracking

up   the rubber hose is not funny the cops
know

how
to work

you over

he used to be one
and the long goodbyes
happened everyday

THE MAD MEN AT CITY LIGHTS

men in bookstores   after five
buttoned downs   shirt
open   at the neck
turned loose among
the poetry   books mumbling
about tits   birds and chicks
and Democrats   if they only had time
for all the books   they have not read
but there's the children
the women waiting   supper's on   the good life
they have made   for them at the table
in bed   the middle age
men who were beatniks
marched with King   every man of a certain age
has marched   with King lived
in a group house ate
vegetables lead the short   happy meatless days
in Cambridge at reading   on the stool throwing
one beer chased with a shot
the poets of the stool
the middle age men   drop in chat
with the poet they touched   Ginsberg gave a wink
Kerouac (o burning angel   wild one of the leather
tight jeans) wrote one book   they read the only bible
of the lost middle age   have a well-thumbed paper
back somewhere these men   of the downtown jazz clubs
and Miles Davis black   and cool I look for them
and their poems they write   the comb-overs
life has led them   to this a stopover
at the remainder tables   a Gary Snyder reading
a love affair   with Gregory Corso
some darkness and mystery
on the flat screen once they   were young and now
they are looking   at the poetry books
before coming home

NOW HE'S GONE

for Harold Madison Jr.

Mr. Butch has clothes for sleeping
his home is on foot city

streets miles long
Mr. Butch is talking to you

like it is himself
give him some change

and he will spare you some
of his time Mr. Butch talks

to sunshine is
thirsty in the parking lots

he's got a lot to say
he's taking the world

into his head My Mr. Butch
is dead he's in the newspaper

Mr. Butch was here
Mr. Butch ain't homeless

he lived in Allston
and now he's gone

THE WAY YOU WERE THAT NIGHT

when jazz
was cool

and the cats
were downtown

they said
the drummer

is a man
white

folks love
the music

is old
jazz clubs

the smoke
in the faces

of the band
"Sweet

Jesus"
man

crazy
sweet pops

head roll
Byrd lives

downtown

www.ingramcontent.com/pod-product-compliance
Lightning Source LLC
LaVergne TN
LVHW050946080826
845145LV00004B/1432

* 9 7 8 0 9 7 9 5 3 1 3 6 1 *